STATES

WISCONSIN

A MyReportLinks.com Book

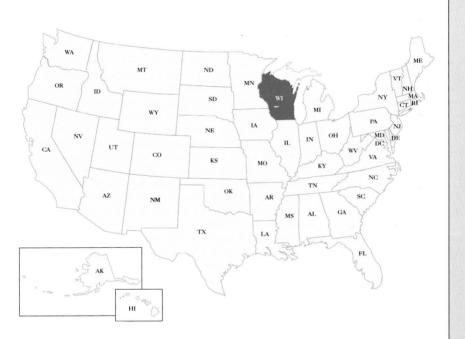

Henry M. Holden

MyReportLinks.com Books

an imprint of

 Enslow Publishers, Inc.

Box 398, 40 Industrial Road
Berkeley Heights, NJ 07922
USA

Back   Forward   Stop   Review   Home   Explore   Favorites   History

MyReportLinks.com Books, an imprint of Enslow Publishers, Inc. MyReportLinks is a trademark of Enslow Publishers, Inc.

Library of Congress Cataloging-in-Publication Data

Holden, Henry M.
 . Wisconsin / Henry M. Holden.
     p. cm. — (States)
Summary: Discusses the land and climate, economy, government, and history of the state of Wisconsin. Includes Internet links to Web sites. Includes bibliographical references and index.
  ISBN 0-7660-5125-0
  1. Wisconsin—Juvenile literature. [1. Wisconsin.] I. Title. II. States (Series : Berkeley Heights, N.J.)
  F581.3 .H65 2003
  977.5—dc21

2002153587

Printed in the United States of America

10 9 8 7 6 5 4 3 2 1

To Our Readers:
Through the purchase of this book, you and your library gain access to the Report Links that specifically back up this book.

The Publisher will provide access to the Report Links that back up this book and will keep these Report Links up to date on **www.myreportlinks.com** for three years from the book's first publication date.

We have done our best to make sure all Internet addresses in this book were active and appropriate when we went to press. However, the author and the Publisher have no control over, and assume no liability for, the material available on those Internet sites or on other Web sites they may link to.

The usage of the MyReportLinks.com Books Web site is subject to the terms and conditions stated on the Usage Policy Statement on **www.myreportlinks.com**.

A password may be required to access the Report Links that back up this book. The password is found on the bottom of page 4 of this book.

Any comments or suggestions can be sent by e-mail to comments@myreportlinks.com or to the address on the back cover.

Photo Credits: © 2001 Robesus, Inc., p. 10 (flag); © Corel Corporation, p. 3; Cave of the Mounds, p. 12; Enslow Publishers, Inc., pp. 1, 17; Library of Congress, pp. 22, 35, 38, 42; MyReportLinks.com Books, p. 4; National Park Service, p. 18; Naturenet.com, p. 14; Wisconsin Department of Tourism, pp. 20, 23, 24, 26, 28, 30, 31, 43; Wisconsin History.org, p. 39; Wisconsin Veterans Museum, p. 40; Wisconsin.gov, p. 33.

Cover Photo: © 1995 PhotoDisc, Inc.

Cover Description: A Wisconsin farm.

Contents

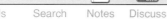

MyReportLinks.com Books
Great Books, Great Links, Great for Research!

MyReportLinks.com Books present the information you need to learn about your report subject. In addition, they show you where to go on the Internet for more information. The pre-evaluated Report Links that back up this book are kept up to date on **www.myreportlinks.com**. With the purchase of a MyReportLinks.com Books title, you and your library gain access to the Report Links that specifically back up that book. The Report Links save hours of research time and link to dozens—even hundreds—of Web sites, source documents, and photos related to your report topic.

Please see "To Our Readers" on the Copyright page for important information about this book, the MyReportLinks.com Books Web site, and the Report Links that back up this book.

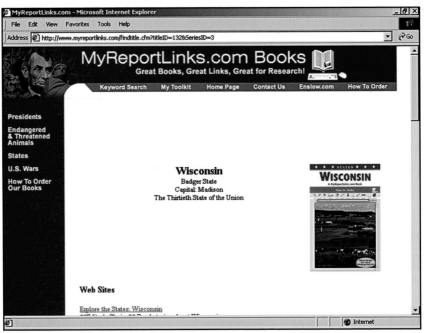

Access:

The Publisher will provide access to the Report Links that back up this book and will try to keep these Report Links up to date on our Web site for three years from the book's first publication date. Please enter **SWI7317** if asked for a password.

The Internet sites described below can be accessed at
http://www.myreportlinks.com

*EDITOR'S CHOICE

▶ **Explore the States: Wisconsin**

This site, provided by the Library of Congress, contains short articles
dealing with historical events in Wisconsin's past. Read about the circus
parade, the Wisconsin Dells, and more!

Link to this Internet site from http://www.myreportlinks.com

*EDITOR'S CHOICE

▶ **Learn About Wisconsin: Just For Kids**

On this site from the Wisconsin State Senate, you can learn about the
state of Wisconsin. Read about the state symbols, the state capitol, and
much more. Be sure to check out "Wisconsin firsts" for information on
laws and policies that were first put into effect in Wisconsin.

Link to this Internet site from http://www.myreportlinks.com

*EDITOR'S CHOICE

▶ **Wisconsin Historical Society**

This site provides a glimpse into the history of Wisconsin. Click on
the "Kids" section for a brief, but informative, time line ranging from
pre-history to the present.

Link to this Internet site from http://www.myreportlinks.com

*EDITOR'S CHOICE

▶ **U.S. Census Bureau: Wisconsin**

The United States Census Bureau provides quick facts and statistics
about Wisconsin. Here you will learn about the state's population,
businesses, and geography.

Link to this Internet site from http://www.myreportlinks.com

*EDITOR'S CHOICE

▶ **The *World Almanac for Kids Online*: Wisconsin**

The *World Almanac for Kids Online* provides essential information
about Wisconsin. Here you will learn about the state's land and
resources, economy, history, government, and much more.

Link to this Internet site from http://www.myreportlinks.com

*EDITOR'S CHOICE

▶ **Wisconsin Milk Marketing Board**

Wisconsin is known as "America's Dairyland." On this site, you can get
information about the milk and cheese industry in Wisconsin. Check
out the "cheesecyclopedia" for "everything you ever wanted to know
about cheese from Wisconsin."

Link to this Internet site from http://www.myreportlinks.com

 The Internet sites described below can be accessed at
http://www.myreportlinks.com

▶ **Aldo Leopold Nature Center**

Aldo Leopold, an author, scholar, and ecologist who helped establish the University of Wisconsin Arboretum, is called the father of the wildlife ecology movement. This site includes a biography of Leopold and facts about the projects going on at this conservation center.

Link to this Internet site from http://www.myreportlinks.com

▶ **Apostle Islands National Lakeshore**

This National Park Service site describes the group of islands at Wisconsin's northern tip known as the Apostle Islands. You can learn about the islands' wildlife and plants and find visitor information.

Link to this Internet site from http://www.myreportlinks.com

▶ **The Cave of the Mounds**

See photos of the Cave of the Mounds in Wisconsin as you read the history of this National Natural Landmark. Also read about Ebenezer Brigham, who owned the farm where the cave was discovered in 1939.

Link to this Internet site from http://www.myreportlinks.com

▶ **Facts About Wisconsin**

On this site from the Wisconsin State government, you can learn about the state capitol as well as Wisconsin's state symbols. Go to "Towns & Cities" to get a list of towns in Wisconsin with a link to each town's respective Web site.

Link to this Internet site from http://www.myreportlinks.com

▶ **50 States: Wisconsin**

At this site, you can find information about Wisconsin's symbols, including the state flower and the state song. Be sure to check out "Fast Facts" for some interesting trivia.

Link to this Internet site from http://www.myreportlinks.com

▶ **Frank Lloyd Wright**

This site gives a biography of famous architect Frank Lloyd Wright, a Wisconsin native. See a list of his accomplishments and quotes as well as books and videos about his works. A photo section shows many of his creations.

Link to this Internet site from http://www.myreportlinks.com

Report Links

The Internet sites described below can be accessed at
http://www.myreportlinks.com

▶ **Georgia O'Keeffe Museum**
The Georgia O'Keeffe Museum site offers a biography of renowned
artist and Wisconsin native Georgia O'Keeffe. View artwork that
includes some of her best-known large-scale depictions of flowers.

Link to this Internet site from http://www.myreportlinks.com

▶ **Harley-Davidson USA: From 1903 Until Now**
It all started in a tiny wooden shed in Wisconsin and has gone on to
become the most recognizable motorcycle manufacturer in the world.
Read the history of Harley-Davidson from its humble beginnings in
1903 to the present.

Link to this Internet site from http://www.myreportlinks.com

▶ **Houdini: A Biographical Chronology**
This Library of Congress site offers a biography of the "Genius of
Escape," Harry Houdini, who immigrated as a child to Wisconsin. Also
offered are links to photographs and documents relating to Houdini.

Link to this Internet site from http://www.myreportlinks.com

▶ **The Keeper's Log**
Learn what life was like to be a lighthouse keeper in the Apostle
Islands in the 1890s. Read the journals of Ella and Emmanuel
Luick, who wrote about their daily lives as lighthouse keepers.

Link to this Internet site from http://www.myreportlinks.com

▶ **Laura Ingalls Wilder 1867–1957**
This biography of author and Wisconsin native Laura Ingalls Wilder
describes not only her life, but that of her parents and siblings and her
husband and his family. A time line of her life is also included.

Link to this Internet site from http://www.myreportlinks.com

▶ **MidContinent Railway and Museum**
Take a virtual tour of the MidContinent Railway and Museum,
located in North Freedom, Wisconsin. View historic photos and
read the history of steam locomotives.

Link to this Internet site from http://www.myreportlinks.com

Report Links

 The Internet sites described below can be accessed at
http://www.myreportlinks.com

▶ Milwaukee Public Museum

Take a virtual tour of the Milwaukee Public Museum, created in 1882. From its humble beginnings to the present, the museum has acquired more than 6,000,000 objects and specimens. Photos and explanations of each exhibit are included.

Link to this Internet site from http://www.myreportlinks.com

▶ Pabst Mansion

Read a brief biography of Captain Frederick Pabst and learn the history of the Pabst Mansion in Milwaukee. Take a photo tour of the mansion known as the "house that beer built."

Link to this Internet site from http://www.myreportlinks.com

▶ Packers.com: The Official Website

The Green Bay Packers Web site includes information on the only professional sports team that is publicly owned. The site includes a history of the team, its coaches, and its stadium as well as statistics from previous NFL seasons.

Link to this Internet site from http://www.myreportlinks.com

▶ Ringling Bros. and Barnum & Bailey

Learn about "The Greatest Show on Earth" and read the history of the seven Ringling brothers, who were from Baraboo, Wisconsin. Biographies of P. T. Barnum and J. A. Bailey are presented, and images are included.

Link to this Internet site from http://www.myreportlinks.com

▶ Stately Knowledge: Wisconsin

The Stately Knowledge Web site provides a brief outline of facts about Wisconsin. You will also find links to additional information about the state.

Link to this Internet site from http://www.myreportlinks.com

▶ Wisconsin

Visit the official tourism web site for Wisconsin and learn about places to visit and things to do in the state. Click on "Virtual Wisconsin" to see panoramic photos of popular attractions.

Link to this Internet site from http://www.myreportlinks.com

Report Links

 The Internet sites described below can be accessed at
http://www.myreportlinks.com

▶ **Wisconsin Department of Natural Resources**

The Wisconsin Department of Natural Resources works to preserve
the natural resources of the state. This site will show you what
preservation work is being done. It also offers photos and information
about hunting, fishing, lakes, and state parks.

Link to this Internet site from http://www.myreportlinks.com

▶ **Wisconsin Electronic Reader**

Stories, essays, photographs, letters, poems, biographies, journals, and
the state's history can all be found on this site that explores Wisconsin's
people and places.

Link to this Internet site from http://www.myreportlinks.com

▶ **Wisconsin Facts**

Did you know that the first ice cream sundae was concocted in
Wisconsin? This site lists facts about the state that include state
symbols, the number of lakes, Wisconsin's foods, the outdoors,
history, and famous people.

Link to this Internet site from http://www.myreportlinks.com

▶ **Wisconsin Music Archives**

The Wisconsin Music Archives, a collection from the 1850s to the
present, contains over 25,000 items representing all Wisconsin
musical traditions. Included are sheet music, folk and ethnic music,
scores, and recordings.

Link to this Internet site from http://www.myreportlinks.com

▶ **Wisconsin State Cranberry Growers Association**

Did you know that the cranberry is one of only three fruits that
are native to North America? Learn this and more about cranberries
and their history in Wisconsin by reading these online brochures.

Link to this Internet site from http://www.myreportlinks.com

▶ **Wisconsin Veterans Museum**

Learn the history of the men and women from Wisconsin who have
served in the United States military by visiting the Wisconsin Veterans
Museum site. The gallery includes images and stories about soldiers
from the Civil War to the present.

Link to this Internet site from http://www.myreportlinks.com

Wisconsin Facts

▶ **Gained Statehood**
May 29, 1848

▶ **Capital**
Madison

▶ **Population**
5,363,675*

▶ **Song**
"On, Wisconsin" (words by J. S. Hubbard and Charles D. Rosa; music by William T. Purdy)

▶ **Motto**
"Forward"

▶ **Nicknames**
Badger State; America's Dairyland

▶ **Animal**
Badger

▶ **Flower**
Wood violet

▶ **Cheese**
Colby

▶ **Tree**
Sugar maple

▶ **Bird**
Robin

▶ **Dance**
Polka

▶ **Rock**
Red granite

▶ **Flag**
On a dark blue field is "Wisconsin" and "1848," the year of statehood. Underneath "Wisconsin" is a scroll with the state's motto, "Forward." Underneath the scroll is a badger, the state animal, sitting on top of a shield, representing Wisconsin's support for the United States. To the right of the shield is a miner, symbolic of those who work on the land, and to the left of the shield is a sailor, symbolic of those who work on the water. A pile of lead representing minerals sits at the feet of the miner. A cornucopia representing farm products rests at the foot of the sailor.

Population reflects the 2000 census.

Chapter 1

The State of Wisconsin

Wisconsin is a land of contrasts, with large wilderness areas, big cities, farms, forests, and manufacturing centers. The northern part of the state features many lakes, including two Great Lakes. Wisconsin's western border is the Mississippi River.

Wisconsin is the twenty-sixth state in total area among the fifty states. About 5.3 million people live in a land area of 54,310 square miles.[1] That is an average of ninety-eight persons per square mile. Most of the northern third of the state, however, is more sparsely populated.

The origin of the name "Wisconsin" is not certain. It is thought to have come from either an American Indian word meaning "gathering of the waters," or one that means "grassy place."

▶ Interesting Places to Visit

The International Crane Foundation, in Baraboo, is the only place in the world where one can see fifteen species of cranes, including the rare whooping crane. Baraboo is also the birthplace of the Ringling Brothers Circus and the home of the Circus World Museum. The Cave of the Mounds, in Blue Mounds, and Crystal Cave, in Spring Valley, are spectacular limestone caves. Two Wisconsin cities, Beeville and Elmwood, each claim to be the UFO capital of the world.[2]

Milwaukee, the state's largest city, features the Milwaukee Mile raceway, which is home to exciting NASCAR stock car races among other events. Milwaukee

Back Forward Stop Review Home Explore Favorites History

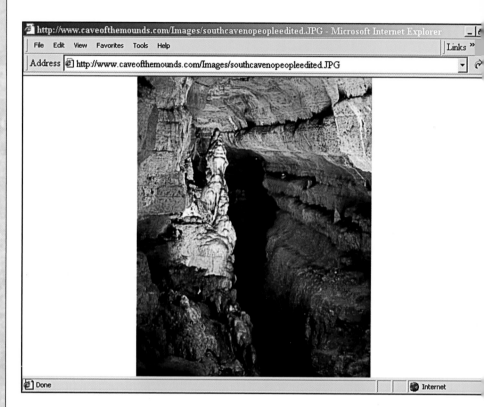

http://www.caveofthemounds.com/Images/southcavenopeopleedited.JPG - Microsoft Internet Explorer

File Edit View Favorites Tools Help   Links »

Address http://www.caveofthemounds.com/Images/southcavenopeopleedited.JPG

Done   Internet

▲ *Cave of the Mounds was discovered by accident in 1939 when some workers at a farm were blasting through a quarry to remove limestone. When they blasted the face of the quarry, they discovered an underground tunnel that led to a huge limestone cavern more than twenty feet high. Cave of the Mounds was opened to the public a year later.*

is also a cultural center, home to the Milwaukee Symphony Orchestra, the Florentine Opera Company, and the Milwaukee Ballet. The Milwaukee Public Museum has a famous dinosaur exhibit and a tropical rain forest exhibit.

▷ Famous Wisconsinites

Frank Lloyd Wright, one of the most influential architects of the twentieth century, was born in Richland Center.

Two of his best-known designs are the S. C. Johnson Building in Racine and the Guggenheim Museum in New York City.

Aldo Leopold, known as the father of the environmental movement, helped establish the University of Wisconsin Arboretum, a center for the study of plants.

Wisconsin has produced famous pilots and military people. General William L. (Billy) Mitchell grew up in Milwaukee. He became the first American to fly over enemy lines in combat, during World War I. He won the Medal of Honor. Major Richard Bong grew up in Poplar. He was America's leading flying "ace" of World War II. He shot down forty enemy planes and won the Medal of Honor. James Lovell, Jr., grew up in Milwaukee. Lovell flew on Gemini and Apollo space missions. Donald K. Slayton, born in Sparta, was one of the original Mercury astronauts.

It seems fitting that since Christopher Sholes was one of the three men who invented the typewriter, and his invention was accomplished in Milwaukee in 1867, many Wisconsin authors have put it to good use, producing Pulitzer Prize–winning works.[3] Thornton Wilder, born in Madison, won Pulitzer Prizes for his novel *The Bridge of San Luis Rey* as well as for his plays *Our Town* and *The Skin of Our Teeth*. Zona Gale, of Portage, won a Pulitzer Prize for her play *Miss Lulu Bett*. Edna Ferber, who grew up in Appleton, also won a Pulitzer Prize for her novel *So Big*. Laura Ingalls Wilder, the author of the famous "Little House" children's books, was born near Pepin, in a log house. At the age of sixty-five, Laura Ingalls Wilder recorded her memories of her childhood on the prairie in her children's books. Those memories were also the basis for the television series *Little House on the Prairie*.

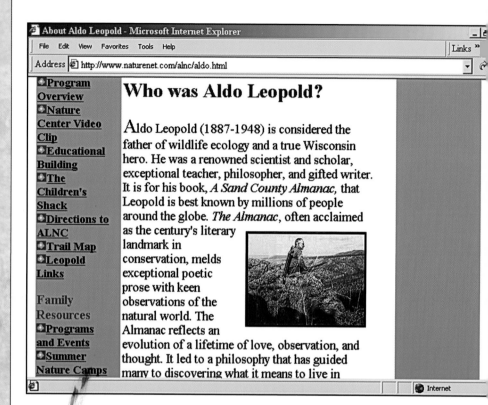

About Aldo Leopold - Microsoft Internet Explorer

File   Edit   View   Favorites   Tools   Help   Links »

Address http://www.naturenet.com/alnc/aldo.html

Program Overview
Nature Center Video Clip
Educational Building
The Children's Shack
Directions to ALNC
Trail Map
Leopold Links

Family Resources
Programs and Events
Summer Nature Camps

Who was Aldo Leopold?

Aldo Leopold (1887-1948) is considered the father of wildlife ecology and a true Wisconsin hero. He was a renowned scientist and scholar, exceptional teacher, philosopher, and gifted writer. It is for his book, *A Sand County Almanac,* that Leopold is best known by millions of people around the globe. *The Almanac*, often acclaimed as the century's literary landmark in conservation, melds exceptional poetic prose with keen observations of the natural world. The Almanac reflects an evolution of a lifetime of love, observation, and thought. It led to a philosophy that has guided many to discovering what it means to live in

Internet

▲ *Aldo Leopold, often credited with being the founder of wildlife ecology, began teaching at the University of Wisconsin in 1928. He was the school's first director of the department of game management, a field he helped to found. He is perhaps best known for his landmark book on ecology,* A Sand County Almanac.

Georgia O'Keeffe, a famous American artist, was born on a farm in Sun Prairie. She is best known for her southwestern scenes and her depictions of flowers.

▶ Stage and Screen

Woodrow (Woody) Herman, born in Milwaukee, was a jazz musician and bandleader. He started his career when he was only six, singing and dancing in local theaters.[4] Wladziu Valentino Liberace, born in West Allis, was a pianist known for his flamboyant costumes. At one time, he was the highest paid entertainer in the United States. Harry Houdini, the famous magician, was raised in Appleton. He was famous for his escapes from handcuffs, straitjackets, and sealed chests.

Wisconsin has also produced its share of famous actors. Spencer Tracy, a native of Milwaukee, was the first actor to win back-to-back Academy Awards, for *Captains Courageous* and *Boys Town.* He was nominated for an Oscar seven times. Orson Welles, from Kenosha, produced, directed, and starred in his first film, *Citizen Kane,* for which he won an Academy Award, and many consider it one of the greatest films ever made.

Don Ameche, born in Kenosha, won an Academy Award for his performance in the film *Cocoon.* Gene Wilder, born in Milwaukee, is an actor, writer, director, and producer. Tyne Daly, a stage, screen, and television actor, was born in Madison. She set an Emmy Award record by winning five Emmys. She has been in more than sixteen television films and over a dozen stage plays.

Sports Legends

George Poage ran track at the University of Wisconsin. In 1904, he became the first African American athlete in history to win a medal (bronze) in the Olympics. Eric Heiden, of Madison, won five Olympic gold medals in speed skating. And although he was born in Brooklyn, New York, Vince Lombardi will forever be linked to the sports world in Wisconsin. As the coach of the National Football League's Green Bay Packers, Lombardi led his team to five NFL championships and victories in the first two Super Bowls.

Chapter 2

Land and Climate

Wisconsin, in the upper midwestern part of the United States, is nearly surrounded by water. Lake Michigan forms its eastern border. Lake Superior and a small portion of Michigan form its northern border. Illinois is its southern land border. The Mississippi River forms most of Wisconsin's western border.

▶ Gifts of the Glaciers

The land that is today Wisconsin was shaped by ice and water. About a million years ago, huge glaciers flowed southward from Canada, covering much of Wisconsin. These giant ice fields crushed trees and mountains and reshaped the land. When the ice melted, water filled the holes cut by the ice, forming rivers, swamps, and about 15,000 lakes. The glaciers also created about 1,400 square miles of inland water.[1]

▶ Lakes and Rivers

Sixteen major rivers, including the Wisconsin and Fox rivers, were formed from the melting ice. Northern Wisconsin has the most lakes per square mile of any area in the world.[2] In the Chequamegon-Nicolet National Forest, there are 430 lakes.[3] The largest inland lake in Wisconsin is Lake Winnebago. It covers more than 137,700 acres.[4] The cities of Oshkosh, Fond du Lac, and Appleton were built on the shores of this lake. The two largest lakes that border Wisconsin are Lake Michigan and

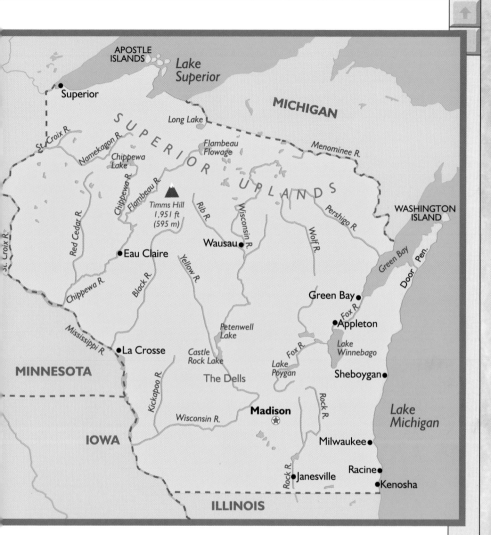

▲ A map of Wisconsin.

Lake Superior. Wisconsin's shoreline on Lake Michigan consists of 381 miles of high bluffs and sandy beaches, while its 292-mile shoreline along Lake Superior is made up of low hills and pebble beaches.[5]

The twenty-two Apostle Islands that jut out into Lake Superior were carved over millions of years by glacial ice, wind, and waves, leaving sandstone cliffs, sea caves, and

miles of sand beaches. There are nine lighthouses on the islands, the largest collection of lighthouses in one area in the United States.[6]

Wisconsin's landscape is also characterized by millions of tons of sand and gravel left behind by glaciers. There is so much sand that former Congressman Henry S. Reuss said, "This country reminds me of an enormous sand box. [It] looks like some giant Neanderthal brought home a load of dirt for his kids to play in."[7] But the sand in Wisconsin has two important uses. First, sand contains silica, and silica is used to make glass. Second, Wisconsin's sand and gravel serve as a filter for groundwater as it percolates down.

The Apostle Islands National Lakeshore contains pristine beaches, sea caves, spectacular wildlife including eagles and bears, and the greatest number of lighthouses in any U.S. National Park.

When ice finished leveling the ancient mountains that were once part of Wisconsin's landscape, the highest point that remained was less than 2,000 feet tall. Today that point is known as Timms Hill, and it is 1,951 feet above sea level. The lowest point in Wisconsin, along the shore of Lake Michigan, is 581 feet above sea level.

Glaciers did not cover the entire state, however. Parts of southern and western Wisconsin that were not affected by glacial melting are called the Driftless Area. There are very few lakes here. In eastern Wisconsin, the Great Lakes Plains extend from Green Bay southward to the state of Illinois. This area contains the richest, most fertile soil and is where most of the farming in Wisconsin takes place. It is also home to Milwaukee, the state's largest city.

Wisconsin's Wildlife

Wisconsin's forests, which cover nearly half the state, are home to bears, white-tailed deer, coyotes, foxes, beavers, muskrats, gophers, prairie mice, and badgers, among other animals. The badger, a symbol of Wisconsin since its days as a territory, is the state animal and the mascot of the University of Wisconsin. The state's many lakes and streams are filled with bass, muskellunge, pickerel, trout, pike, and sturgeon. Birds found in Wisconsin include ducks, geese, pheasants, and ruffed grouse, among other game birds, as well as loons and other waterfowl, which breed on the lakes found in the northern parts of the state. Chickadees, nuthatches, wrens, robins, warblers, and swallows are also found in Wisconsin.

Climate

Wisconsin's climate can reach extremes of heat and cold. Southern Wisconsin features warm summers, while

◁ *The shoreline in Squaw Bay, in northern Wisconsin, after a snowfall.*

the summer temperatures elsewhere in the state are more moderate. Winters in northern Wisconsin are severe, with heavy snowfalls—sometimes as much as one hundred inches of snow annually. In 1978, Milwaukee received eighty inches of snow, and temperatures remained below freezing for fifty-two days in a row. In the southern part of the state, the climate is milder. It may only get about thirty inches of snow a year. The average spring temperature in Wisconsin is 45°F. In the summer months, the temperature may reach into the 90s. Winter temperatures average about 20°F, but temperatures can fall below zero. The Great Lakes also affect Wisconsin's climate. They create milder weather in the winter and cooler weather in the summer along the coast. The coldest recorded temperature in Wisconsin was –54°F in 1922, at Danbury. The highest recorded temperature in the state was 114°F in 1936, at Wisconsin Dells.

Economy

The French, who arrived in the seventeenth century, were the first Europeans to explore and settle the lands that are today Wisconsin. In 1660, a French trading post and a Catholic mission were established near what is now Ashland. Soon, French fur trappers from Canada entered the region in greater numbers, and fur trading became the foundation of Wisconsin's early economy. The first Americans to arrive began mining lead, used in buckshot for guns and in paint.

▶ Trapping, Trading, Beer, Bikes, and Sausages

Milwaukee, Wisconsin's largest city, started out as a trading post. By the late nineteenth century, Milwaukee had become "the beer capital of the world" after its breweries, begun in the mid-1800s as small, local operations by German immigrants, began expanding and selling their products nationwide. Soon, Pabst, Miller, and Schlitz, three of Milwaukee's largest breweries, were known across the country, and, later, throughout the world. Milwaukee also became famous for its German-style sausages.

Milwaukee is the place where one of the world's largest and most popular makers of motorcycles had its beginnings. In 1903, in a ten-by-fifteen-foot wooden shed, William S. Harley and Arthur Davidson built a motorized bicycle to be used as a racer. With the help of Davidson's brother Walter and Henry Meyer, a childhood friend, they began the Harley-Davidson Motor Company,

Back   Forward   Stop   Review   Home   Explore   Favorites   History

File   Edit   View   Favorites   Tools   Help   Links »

Address http://www.americaslibrary.gov/cgi-bin/page.cgi/es/wi/hog_1

★Home ★About this site ★Help   The Library of Congress

America's Story from America's Library

Meet Amazing Americans | Jump Back in Time | **Explore the States** | Join America at Play | See, Hear and Sing

Explore the States ▸ Wisconsin

Harley-Davidson: "Coming Home"
A Local Legacy
Have you ever seen someone ride a hog? No, not a pig, a Harley-Davidson motorcycle!

In 1903, this little one-room building was the birthplace of the world's most famous motorcycle company -- Harley-Davidson. On its 95th anniversary in 1998, more than 100,000 Harley-Davidson fans gathered in Milwaukee to celebrate. Many riders took part in five fund-raising rides, which left from

The original 1903 Harley-Davidson motorcycle factory

Click for enlargement and credits

http://www.americaslibrary.gov/cgi-bin/page.cgi/jp   Internet

▲ *The original Harley-Davidson motorcycle "factory" was this small wooden shed in Milwaukee.*

still based in Milwaukee but with dealerships around the world.

▶ Agriculture in America's Dairyland

Wisconsin, with abundant rich farmland, is one of the leading agricultural states in the United States with more than $5.5 billion in farm-product sales per year. There are about 77,000 farms in Wisconsin, with an average size of about 210 acres. Dairy farming is important to the state's economy. In fact, Wisconsin is known as "America's Dairyland" because it ranks first in the country in cheese production and second in milk and butter production. There are about 1.5 million dairy cows in Wisconsin.[1] They produce a year's supply of milk for 42 million people.[2] Most of the milk is made into cheese products. The milk produced in Wisconsin provides enough butter for 68 million people and enough cheese for 86 million.[3]

Wisconsin is also among the top five producers of snap beans, green peas, and cabbage in the United States. It leads the nation in corn grown for feed and is third in the nation in the production of carrots and potatoes.[4] Cranberries, one of only three fruits native to North America (the others are blueberries and Concord grapes) are Wisconsin's number-one fruit crop, and the state produces over 50 percent of the nation's cranberry crop.[5] Wisconsin farmers also raise cattle, sheep, and pigs.

▲ Just some of the products made from milk that comes from Wisconsin, "America's Dairyland."

Wisconsin's largest fruit crop is cranberries, seen here after harvesting.

▶ Other Industries

The paper and lumber industries, food processing industry, and motor vehicle manufacturing are also important to Wisconsin's economy. Wisconsin ranks eleventh among all states in manufacturing. The state leads the nation in the production of low-horsepower gasoline engines, power cranes, shovel hoists, and mining machinery.[6] Some of its better-known products are Oshkosh B'Gosh children's clothing, Oscar Mayer hot dogs, and John Deere tractors. Racine is the home of S. C. Johnson and Sons, Inc., a leading manufacturer of cleaning products and other products for the home.

▶ Shipbuilding and the Great Lakes Ports

The Great Lakes were especially important to Wisconsin's early economy. Four of Wisconsin's five largest cities are on Lake Michigan. Manitowoc, on Lake Michigan, is where

Wisconsin's shipbuilding industry began. After World War I, Manitowoc was known for its production of freighters, car ferries, and oil tankers. During World War II, submarines were built there. Today, the port ships grain and malt. Shipbuilding and repair of the Great Lakes freighters is still a major industry there.

The port of Milwaukee was a major port of entry for immigrants in the 1840s. It was for a time the world's leading wheat market and flour mill. The port of Milwaukee is still a center for bulk freight and European products.

The port of Superior ships ore and grain. It is also a container cargo depot for the Burlington Northern and Santa Fe Railroad. Shipbuilding in Superior began in the 1850s with lake schooners. During World War II, Liberty ships (cargo ships that carried much-needed war supplies) were built there.

Sturgeon Bay began as a limestone and lumber shipping port. It then became a shipbuilding center. Today one company builds and repairs ships as large as the 1,000-foot lake freighters.

Green Bay shipped ice for Chicago's meatpacking trade until the 1920s. The modern port of Green Bay handles consumer goods from the Fox Valley paper manufacturers. When the St. Lawrence Seaway was completed, it made seaports out of Wisconsin's Great Lakes cities, enabling ships to sail from cities such as Green Bay directly to the Atlantic Ocean.

► The Importance of Wisconsin's Rivers

Wisconsin's rivers play an essential role in the state's economy. The Wisconsin River, which flows for about 430 miles through the state, is one of Wisconsin's most important natural resources. It begins at Lac Vieux

Desert, on the Wisconsin-Michigan border, and ends at Prairie du Chien, where it empties into the Mississippi River. At Portage, the Wisconsin River is connected to the Fox River and Lake Michigan by a short canal. Parts of the river are used for recreation, such as sport fishing and boating. Other parts are used for farming and logging. With more than 15 million acres of forests in Wisconsin, the river serves as an important waterway to transport the logs that are used to make paper products. Wisconsin ranks second in paper production out of the forty-seven states that produce paper in the United States.[7] The major paper mills are found in Green Bay and along the Fox River.

The Portage Canal connects the Wisconsin and Fox rivers. The canal is also on the Ice Age National Scenic Trail, which runs along the edges of the glacier that covered Wisconsin during the last ice age.

The headwaters of the Fox River begin in Waukesha County. The Fox River is one of the few rivers in North America to flow north from its source, which is in Portage, in central Wisconsin. The river drops about two hundred feet along its route to Green Bay, making it a good source of hydroelectric power. In 1882, the first hydroelectric plant in the United States opened in Appleton, on the Fox River. Electricity is generated by the power of water coming through dams built along the river, and that electricity is then used to power the paper mills on the river.

▷ Education

Watertown, Wisconsin, was the first city in the United States to open a kindergarten. The oldest university in Wisconsin is Nashotah House. It opened in 1842 as an Episcopal seminary. Carroll College, in Waukesha, opened in 1846. It is the oldest private college in Wisconsin. The huge University of Wisconsin opened in 1849. It has thirteen campuses and thirteen two-year colleges. Wisconsin's private institutions include three universities, seventeen colleges, four technical and professional schools, and four theological seminaries. Two American Indian tribes in Wisconsin have public community colleges. Wisconsin's 432 school districts consistently score higher than the national average and higher than the average of schools in other midwestern states.[8]

▷ Transportation

Wisconsin has more than 110,000 miles of highways and other paved roads.[9] Wisconsin was the first state to identify its highways with numbers. Many of its big cities are served by bus lines.

▲ Pattison State Park is home to Little Manitou Falls. The park is one of ninety state parks in Wisconsin.

Tourism

Tourism is a $10 billion industry in the state of Wisconsin. Wisconsin's forest and water resources have made it the top vacation area in the Midwest. The Wisconsin Dells area (made up of the city of Wisconsin Dells and the village of Lake Delton) attracts many tourists to its indoor and outdoor water parks and themed hotels. Noah's Ark, covering more than sixty-five acres, is the world's largest water park.[10] Guests can visit theme parks that make them feel as if they were in Africa or Alaska and never leave the Wisconsin Dells.

Wisconsin's Great River Road winds along the Mississippi River for about 250 miles on Wisconsin's western border. The Great River Road is home to more than fifty local parks and beaches and twelve state and three national recreational areas. Observation decks at four locks and dams allow tourists to watch the barges and riverboats pass through the locks. Visitors can also see steamboats like the *Delta Queen* on the river and spot bald eagles along this route.

Sports and Recreation

With Lakes Michigan and Superior, the Mississippi River, thousands of inland lakes, and 33,000 miles of rivers, it is easy to see why boating, jet skiing, and sportfishing are popular in Wisconsin. Winter in Wisconsin offers ice fishing and ice sailing on many of its lakes. There are about six thousand state-owned campsites in Wisconsin and 25,000 miles of skiing and snowmobile trails.[11]

Every February about six thousand people take part in a thirty-one-mile cross-country ski marathon called the American Birkebeiner. It is the largest cross-country ski

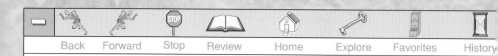

▲ *Wisconsinites love their Green Bay Packers, seen here at practice in warmer weather than their games are often played in.*

race in the United States, and it is used to qualify athletes for the Olympic Games.

Wisconsin has three major professional sports teams: the Milwaukee Brewers baseball team, the Green Bay Packers football team, and the Milwaukee Bucks basketball team. Milwaukee is also home to a professional soccer team and a minor-league hockey team.

Oshkosh holds the world's largest aviation event, EAA AirVenture, which attracts more than 2,000 airplanes and 750,000 people for the weeklong fly-in. Wausau hosts the World Cup Kayak Races, which take place on the Wisconsin River.

Government

In 1848, Wisconsin became the thirtieth state admitted to the Union. The state is divided into seventy-two counties. The state capital is Madison.

Throughout its history, Wisconsin has been known for progressive political leadership and pioneering social

▲ The State Capitol, in Madison, is the only state capitol to be built on an isthmus—it is situated on a narrow strip of land between Lake Monona and Lake Mendota.

legislation. It was the first state to provide pensions for the blind, aid to dependent children, and old-age assistance. Wisconsin was also the first state to create an unemployment compensation law and the first to enact an injured workers' compensation law.

Constitution

Wisconsin's constitution divides the powers of the government between the executive, legislative, and judicial branches. This provides a system of checks and balances, preventing one branch from gaining too much power.

The Executive Branch

The head of the executive branch is the governor, who is elected to a four-year term. He or she signs bills into law or vetoes them. As the state's chief executive, the governor represents all the people. The governor has sole power to extradite, or transfer, a person charged with a criminal offense to another state. He or she may exercise executive clemency by granting a pardon or may commute the sentence of a convicted criminal.

The Legislative Branch

Wisconsin's legislature is the law-making branch of the state's government. There are two houses in the legislature: The upper house is the senate, and the lower house is the general assembly. There are thirty-three members of the senate and ninety-nine members of the general assembly. Senators serve four-year terms, and assembly members serve two-year terms. On the national level, Wisconsin has two U.S. senators and nine members of the House of Representatives. The state casts eleven electoral votes in presidential elections.

Wisconsin.gov - Capitol Facts - Wisconsin State Capitol Virtual Tour - Microsoft Internet Explorer

e Edit View Favorites Tools Help   Links »

Address http://www.wisconsin.gov/state/capfacts/supreme_court_s.html   Go

apitol Home
apitol Tour
rtual Reality Tour
oto Tour
story
ap View
elp
ortal Home
overnment
ablic Services
usiness
ducation
isconsin Facts
ealth & Safety
elocation
siting

Wisconsin State Capitol Supreme Court

- Rotunda
- Lantern Balcony
- Capitol Exterior
- Supreme Court
- Governor's
  Conference Room
- Senate Chamber
- Assembly
  Chamber
- North
  Hearing Room

Supreme Court

The Supreme Court Room is located on the second floor of the east wing of the State Capitol. Upon entering, visitors will be impressed by its dignified beauty. Such a room is befitting for the Supreme Court for it is here, where the final interpretation of State law is made.

Wisconsin State Supreme Court Justices and the Fourth District Court of Appeals use the Supreme Court Room for oral arguments. The Supreme Court meets in this room two to three times per month, from September through June. The remainder of the year, the justices work on

Internet

▲ *Wisconsin's supreme court meets in this room on the second floor of the east wing of the State Capitol.*

▷ Judicial Branch

The highest court in the state's judicial branch is the supreme court. It hears appeals from lower courts. The supreme court selects the cases it hears based on specific guidelines. The supreme court justices are appointed to ten-year terms. Other courts include the circuit courts and appellate court. The circuit courts are where most trials take place. The appellate court hears appeals of decisions from the circuit courts.

▷ Famous Wisconsin Leaders

Wisconsin has been home to many political leaders. William H. Rehnquist, born in Milwaukee, is the chief justice of the United States.

Golda Meir, whose family emigrated from Russia to the United States in 1906, grew up in Milwaukee. In 1921, she moved to what was then Palestine (today Israel). In 1948, she was part of the People's Council that helped establish the state of Israel.[1] In 1969, Golda Meir became the prime minister of Israel and served in that position until 1974.

Carrie Chapman Catt, an American suffragist, was born in Ripon. She was president of the National American Woman Suffrage Association and led the campaign to win women's suffrage, or the right to vote. She also organized the League of Women Voters.

A member of the Republican Party, Robert La Follette was elected a U.S. representative from Wisconsin to Congress in 1884. But La Follette disagreed with his party's policies and broke with its leadership. Elected Wisconsin's governor in 1900, he led a movement for social and economic reform. He believed that government should rely on experts in economics, administration, and politics. Under his leadership, Wisconsin enacted social and economic programs, including a minimum wage law for women and children and a workers' compensation law to benefit people injured on the job, among other programs. Later other states adopted similar laws. La Follette also signed laws for direct primary elections, tax reform, railroad rate control, and other progressive measures that were recommended by academics from the University of Wisconsin. These progressive measures became known as

Carrie Chapman Catt, born in Ripon, Wisconsin, was a suffragist and peace advocate who led the fight for women's suffrage by advocating a federal amendment to the Constitution.

the "Wisconsin Idea." La Follette became a U.S. senator in 1906 and ran for the presidency in 1924 on the Progressive Party ticket.

Another Wisconsin politician became notorious for his persecution of members of the federal government during the 1950s. Republican senator Joseph McCarthy began accusing members of the State Department and the U.S. Army command of being Communists at a time when the Cold War was at its height. His accusations led to hearings in which many people's reputations were damaged even though McCarthy was able to offer no proof that the accused were Communists. Eventually the Senate censured McCarthy for his abuse of power.

Chapter 5

History

Thousands of years ago, the first people who came to North America crossed a land bridge that once connected Asia to North America. Some of them settled in Wisconsin about 9,400 years ago.[1] We know little about these ancient people except that they were hunters and left behind the stone tools they used to scrape hides from animals for clothing and shelter.

As the climate became warmer, other American Indians moved to Wisconsin. Some of them used copper tools and were thus called the old Copper Culture Indians. The copper for those tools was found around Lake Superior. The Chippewa Indians called this lake "Gitchee Gumee." Some remains of their ancient mines, and fires in which the copper was melted, have been found in Green Bay.

▶ Early Explorations

The first European explorer to reach the land that would become Wisconsin was a Frenchman, Jean Nicolet, during his search for a northwest passage to China and India. Nicolet sailed across Lake Michigan and landed in Green Bay in 1634. He claimed the land for France. Later French explorers Jacques Marquette and Louis Joliet traveled from Green Bay up the Fox River to the Wisconsin River and then to the Mississippi River. When the first European explorers arrived in Wisconsin, they found many tribes of American Indians. The Winnebago,

Chippewa, Dakota, Fox, Sauk, and Menominee were living there.

French, British, and American Colonialism

In 1763, following the French and Indian War, the French lost Wisconsin to Great Britain. With the end of the Revolutionary War, Wisconsin became part of the United States. In 1787, under the Northwest Ordinance, Wisconsin became part of the Northwest Territory, so called because it lay north and west of the Ohio River. Ohio, Indiana, Illinois, Michigan, and Wisconsin were later created from the Northwest Territory. However, Great Britain, which continued to dominate the fur trade in the area, retained control of Wisconsin until after the War of 1812. The region was governed as part of the territories of Indiana, Illinois, and Michigan until 1836, when it became a separate territory.

Early American Settlers

The first large wave of American settlers arrived in Wisconsin in the 1820s, attracted by the lead mining boom. Many miners did not take the time to build houses for themselves. Instead, they dug holes in the ground, like badgers, to rest at night. Soon they came to be called "badgers," giving Wisconsin its nickname, the Badger State.

The Black Hawk War

In 1804, the Sauk and Fox Indians had been moved out of Illinois when they signed a treaty designed to open up the lands for white settlement. The Sauk and Fox were resettled west of the Mississippi River. But a chief named Black Hawk, who claimed the treaty was not valid, returned east

◁ Black Hawk, Chief of the Sauk and Fox, whose tribe was massacred at the Bad Axe River in 1832. In 1989, the State of Wisconsin passed Assembly Resolution 16, which was an apology to tribal officials of the Sauk and Fox nations for the Bad Axe Massacre.

with his people to Illinois in 1832. The government called out troops, and Black Hawk fought back. He defeated a large force of troops and then moved his band north to Wisconsin. The terms of the treaty, however, had transferred all land titles in Wisconsin to the U.S. government, so more troops were sent to remove Black Hawk and his people from Wisconsin. The troops surrounded Black Hawk's band, and the Indians fought back, but they were soon out of food and ammunition. Even though Black Hawk flew the flag of surrender, almost all of his band, including women and children, were killed. Black Hawk himself escaped, but later surrendered. This battle became known as the Bad Axe Massacre. Of the sixteen hundred Indians who had traveled with Black Hawk, only a handful survived. The Black Hawk War marked the last Indian uprising east of the Mississippi River.

▷ The Wisconsin Territory

In 1836, Wisconsin became a separate territory, and soon waves of settlers arrived, attracted by good farmland.

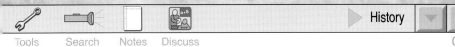
By 1840, there were about thirty thousand settlers in the state.[2] Railroads began to be built there around 1850, to serve the growing wheat harvests and mines. Soon, Wisconsin ranked second in the nation in wheat production.

Statehood, Slavery, and the Civil War

Wisconsin's settlers, fearing higher taxes and strict government, rejected statehood four times before 1848, the year Wisconsin finally became a state. In that year, the newly formed Free Soil Party, which opposed slavery in new territories, was popular in Wisconsin. Living in a Northern state where slavery was not legal, Wisconsin's citizens were

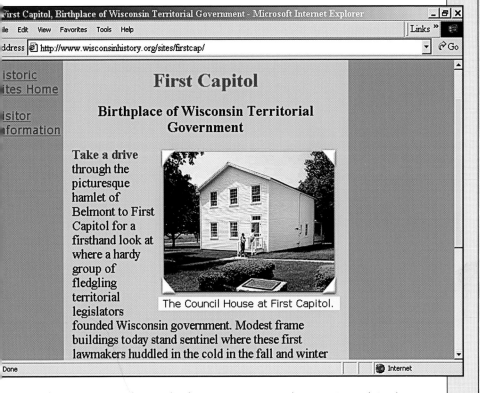

The territorial capital of Wisconsin was Belmont. Pictured is the Council House, where the territory's leaders formed Wisconsin's first government.

opposed to the practice. The town of Ripon, Wisconsin, is generally regarded as the birthplace of the Republican Party in 1854, which was formed in response to the Kansas-Nebraska Act passed that year. That act established the territories of Kansas and Nebraska, but instead of prohibiting slavery there, as the Missouri Compromise had provided for in 1820, the decision to allow slavery or ban it was left up to the settlers. Wisconsin's abolitionists thus played a large part in forming the new Republican Party.

As the debate over slavery finally led to the Civil War in 1861, Wisconsin's citizens responded by rallying to the

Wisconsin's citizens were anxious to heed the Union's call, but not all its soldiers were properly dressed for battle. Unfortunately, there was not enough blue cloth to go around, so gray cloth was substituted for the uniforms of eight Wisconsin regiments—who marched into war dressed in the colors of the Confederate army.

Union cause, furnishing the Union army with 96,000 soldiers. About 130 Wisconsin men served in the U.S. Navy and 165 with the African-American regiments. A group of Wisconsin soldiers formed the Eagle Regiment, with a bald eagle mascot named Old Abe. Old Abe led the regiment into many battles and flew over the troops. He was never wounded, and after the war, the state gave Old Abe a place of honor in the state capitol.

During and following the war, railroads began to link Wisconsin with the East, and the state's meatpacking and brewing industries flourished. By the 1870s, the state's dairy industry became prominent.

Peshtigo Fire

On October 8, 1871—the same day as the great Chicago fire—a terrible fire broke out in Peshtigo, Wisconsin. The summer had been hot and dry, and there was no rain during the fall. The people in the town of Peshtigo were worried about the forests surrounding the town, since there had been reports of forest fires in many areas. Suddenly, the town seemed to burst into flames. Many people escaped the fire by jumping into the river. The fire burned all night. By morning, it had killed about twelve hundred people, about five times as many people as had perished in the Chicago fire, and it had burned an area forty miles long by ten miles wide, a much larger area than the village of Peshtigo itself.[3]

The Progressive Movement

Wisconsin's political leaders of the late nineteenth and early twentieth centuries led the country in some of the most progressive reforms of the time. Political views in the state were more liberal than those in other midwestern

◁ *Robert M. La Follette, a leading member of the Progressive Party, was a U.S. representative, governor of Wisconsin, and presidential candidate. As the state's governor, La Follette signed into law some of the most progressive measures of the time, and those laws were soon adopted by other states.*

states. Milwaukee politics were for years dominated by a "practical socialism" that helped city government to run efficiently. Early in the twentieth century, the Progressive movement, led by former governor and senator Robert La Follette, gained strength. In 1924, La Follette ran for the presidency on the Progressive ticket. In the 1920s and 1930s, social reforms such as an old-age pension act and an unemployment compensation act that were developed in Wisconsin became models for federal programs.

▷ Wisconsin's Role in World War II

During the 1940s, Wisconsin played a major role in wartime shipbuilding. Twenty-eight submarines were built on Lake Michigan. Test dives took place in Lake Michigan, and the submarines were barged down the Mississippi River to the Gulf of Mexico.

More than one hundred vessels including landing craft, minesweepers, and submarine chasers for the war were built in Wisconsin. About 332,200 Wisconsin men and women served in the military. Wisconsin's wartime economy flourished in the southeastern part of the state, where factories produced tanks and trucks, and in the north, where paper mills produced the paper that was made into books, maps, and other products for the soldiers. The state's manufacturing centers continued to do well late into the twentieth century even while other states experienced a decline in manufacturing.

Modern Challenges

Wisconsin moves into the twenty-first century faced with some of the problems that other states face. It has to find jobs for its unemployed, provide decent housing and good schools, and clean up air and water pollution. Its four nuclear power plants produce electricity with less pollution than results from the burning of fossil fuels.

In 1993, Milwaukee's drinking water became polluted with harmful bacteria. Hundreds of people became ill,

▲ The Flambeau River in Price County offers twenty-three rapids for whitewater-rafting enthusiasts. The state is dedicated to protecting its natural resources for its current residents and for future generations.

and some died. Some people thought that the bacteria came from farms whose animal wastes were washed into rivers by rain. Rivers such as the Fox River also carry pollutants from the paper industry into Lake Michigan. The river is badly contaminated with thousands of pounds of toxic chemicals called PCBs (polychlorinated biphenyls). In some areas of Wisconsin, the groundwater is too polluted to drink. In 1955, when groundwater supplies were used up, the city of Green Bay built a pipeline thirty-one miles long to get drinking water from Lake Michigan. Other cities in Brown County, on Lake Michigan, are considering building a pipeline to the lake because their groundwater supplies have been used up.[4]

Wisconsin is also looking for ways to provide safe drinking water while not harming the farming economy. And the state has spent more than $95 million cleaning up hazardous waste sites.[5]

Dairy farmers are also facing challenges to their practices. A substance known as bovine growth hormone (BGH) is given to some cows to help them produce more milk. The government says that BGH is not harmful to people who drink the milk from such cows, but others disagree. Dairy farms that use BGH are able to increase their productivity, and farms that do not use it may go out of business.

What seems likely is that the state of Wisconsin, which has long been a leader in social and political reform, will come up with new and progressive ways to deal with these challenges and others that come its way.

Chapter Notes

Chapter 1. The State of Wisconsin

1. *The United States Census Bureau,* "State and County Quick Facts—Wisconsin, 2000," <http://quickfacts.census.gov/qfd/states/55000.html> (September 3, 2002).

2. Wisconsin Department of Tourism Web site, "Wisconsin Tourism Facts—Vital Statistics,"<http://agency.travelwisconsin.com/PR/Tourism_Facts/Facts.shtm#VITALSTATISTICS> (April 15, 2003).

3. Martin Hintz and Daniel Hintz, *Wisconsin Off the Beaten Trail* (Guilford, Conn.: The Globe Pequot Press, 2002), p. 157.

4. *The Jazz Institute of Chicago,* "Woody Herman," n.d., <http://jazzinstituteofchicago.org/index.asp?target=/jazzgram/articles/herman-obituary.asp> (September 3, 2002).

Chapter 2. Land and Climate

1. Wisconsin Department of Tourism Web site, "Wisconsin Tourism Facts—Vital Statistics,"<http://agency.travelwisconsin.com/PR/Tourism_Facts/Facts.shtm#VITALSTATISTICS> (April 15, 2003).

2. Anne La Bastille, "On the Trail of Wisconsin's Ice Age," *National Geographic,* August 1977, p. 189.

3. Martin Hintz and Daniel Hintz, *Wisconsin Off the Beaten Trail* (Guilford, Conn.: The Globe Pequot Press, 2002), p. 78.

4. Ibid., p. XIII.

5. Ibid., p. 137.

6. *The National Park Service,* Apostle Islands National Lakeshore, "Lighthouses of the Apostle Islands," n.d., <http://www.nps.gov/apis/table.htm> (September 3, 2002).

7. La Bastille, p. 203.

Chapter 3. Economy

1. Martin Hintz and Daniel Hintz, *Wisconsin Off the Beaten Trail* (Guilford, Conn.: The Globe Pequot Press, 2002), p. 18.

2. Wisconsin Department of Tourism Web site, "Wisconsin Tourism Facts—Vital Statistics,"<http://agency.travelwisconsin.com/PR/Tourism_Facts/Facts.shtm#VITALSTATISTICS> (April 15, 2003).

3. Ibid.

4. Ibid.

5. *Wisconsin State Cranberry Growers Association,* "History," n.d., <http://www.wiscran.org/history.html> (September 3, 2002).

6. Wisconsin Department of Tourism Web site.

7. *RiverRoads.com,* "Wisconsin," n.d., <http://www.riverroads.com/cgi-bin/masterframereunion.cgi?http%3A//www.riverroads.com/states/wisc/wisc.html> (September 3, 2002).

8. Wisconsin Department of Tourism Web site.

9. Hintz, p. 136.

10. Wisconsin Department of Tourism Web site.

11. Hintz, p. 80.

Chapter 4. Government

1. *Women's International Center,* "Golda Meir," n.d., <http://www.wic.org/bio/gmeir.htm> (September 3, 2002).

Chapter 5. History

1. Anne La Bastille, "On the Trail of Wisconsin's Ice Age," *National Geographic,* August 1977, p. 199.

2. Martin Hintz and Daniel Hintz, *Wisconsin Off the Beaten Trail* (Guilford, Conn.: The Globe Pequot Press, 2002), p. XIV.

3. Deana C. Hipke, *The Great Peshtigo Fire of 1871,* n.d., <http://www.peshtigofire.info/> (March 10, 2003).

4. *Fox River Watch, a Project of the Clean Water Action Council,* "History of the Fox River and Green Bay," n.d., <http://www.foxriverwatch.com/history_fox_river_green_bay_1.html> (September 3, 2002).

5. *Ground Water Protection Council Online,* "Wisconsin's Ground Water Conditions," p. 101, n.d, <http://www.gwpc.org/gwreport/Acrobat/Wisconsin.pdf> (March 5, 2003).

Further Reading

Barenblat, Rachel. *Wisconsin: The Badger State.* Milwaukee: Gareth Stevens, Inc., 2002.

Butler, Dori Hillestad, and Eileen Dawson. *W Is for Wisconsin.* Black Earth, Wis.: Trails Books, 1998.

Capstone Press Staff. *Wisconsin.* Minnetonka, Minn.: Capstone Press, Incorporated, 1997.

Chamberlain, Dolores. *River Stories: Growing Up on the Wisconsin.* Madison, Wis.: Prairie Oak Press, Inc., 2000.

Hintz, Martin. *Wisconsin Portraits: 55 People Who Made a Difference.* Black Earth, Wis.: Trails Media Group, Inc., 2000.

Kavanagh, James. *Wisconsin Birds.* Chandler, Ariz.: Waterford Press, Ltd., 1999.

Leopold, Aldo. *A Sand County Almanac.* New York: Oxford University Press, Inc., 2001.

Ling, Bettina. *Wisconsin.* Chicago: Children's Press, 2002.

Shull, Jodie A. *Georgia O'Keeffe: Legendary American Painter.* Berkeley Heights, N.J.: Enslow Publishers, Inc., 2003.

Thompson, Kathleen. *Wisconsin: Portrait of America.* Austin, Tex.: Steck-Vaughn, 1996.

Wade, Mary D., et al. *Homesteading on the Plains: Daily Life in the Land of Laura Ingalls Wilder.* Brookfield, Conn.: Millbrook Press, 1997.